NEP 2020: WHAT EVERY TEACHER SHOULD KNOW?

DR DHEERAJ MEHROTRA

Made with ♥ on the Notion Press Platform
www.notionpress.com

Contents

Preface

Education drives progress and shapes people and nations. The National Education Policy (NEP) 2020 transforms India's education system by emphasising flexibility, diversity, and innovation. It transforms learning into a comprehensive, student-centred, skill-based approach to prepare students for 21st-century issues.

Teachers are key to this change. Competency-based education, transdisciplinary learning, technological integration, critical thinking, and creativity are priorities of NEP 2020. The strategy emphasises ECCE, FLN, continual professional development, and outcome-based learning. It requires a paradigm shift in teaching methods, evaluation procedures, and the roles of educators in promoting joyful and meaningful learning.

NEP 2020: What Every Teacher Should Know is a comprehensive guide for educators to understand, interpret, and apply the policy's key elements. It informs and empowers educators to shape India's education future. This book will help teachers, administrators, and academic professionals understand NEP 2020 and how to apply it in the classroom.

Let us embrace this transition with enthusiasm, adaptability, and a devotion to providing our children with the most significant education that develops their abilities, skills, and aspirations. To make NEP 2020 a success, teachers must apply it.

Happy Teaching!

www.authordheerajmehrotra.com

I

100 Key Points

The National Education Policy (NEP) 2020 is a transformative framework for education in India.

Let us understand the 100 key points that every teacher should know about NEP 2020:

Foundational Principles

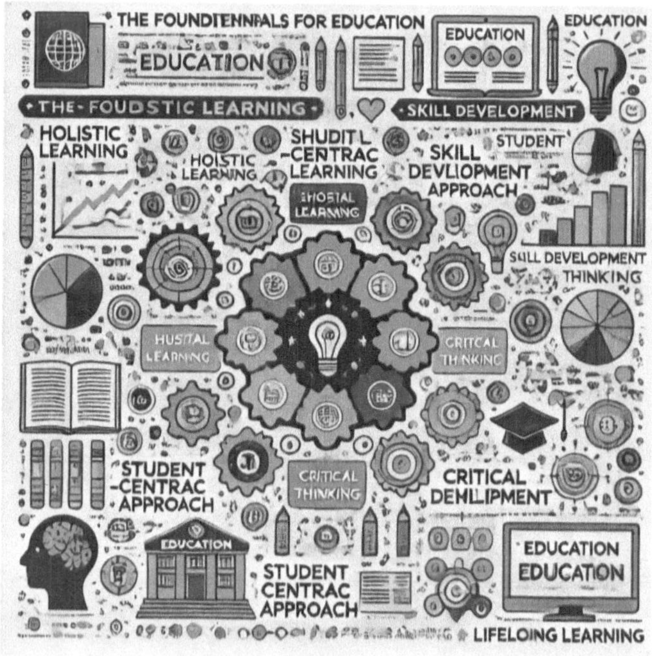

1. Focus on equitable and inclusive education.

2. Emphasis on holistic development of learners.

3. Integration of Indian culture and values into education.

4. Promotion of multilingualism and Indian languages.

5. Shift from rote learning to critical thinking and creativity.

6. Emphasis on lifelong learning.

7. Alignment with the United Nations Sustainable Development Goals (SDGs).

School Education

8. 5+3+3+4 curricular structure replacing the 10+2 system.

9. Foundational Stage (ages 3-8): Focus on

play-based learning.

10. Preparatory Stage (ages 8-11): Basic literacy and numeracy.

11. Middle Stage (ages 11-14): Experiential learning in sciences, math, arts, etc.

12. Secondary Stage (ages 14-18): Multidisciplinary study with flexibility.

13. Universalization of education from preschool to secondary level.

14. 100% Gross Enrolment Ratio (GER) by 2030.

15. National Mission on Foundational Literacy and Numeracy.

16. Bagless days for hands-on learning and vocational training.

17. 10 bagless days per year for experiential learning.

18. Vocational education from Grade 6 onwards.

19. Coding and computational thinking were introduced in Grade 6.

20. Reduction in curriculum content to focus on core concepts.

21. No hard separation between arts, sciences, and vocational streams.

22. Board exams to test core competencies rather than rote learning.

23. Two attempts for board exams to reduce stress.

24. School complexes for resource sharing among schools.

25. Integration of technology in teaching and learning.

26. National Curriculum Framework (NCF) to be revised.

27. Teacher training to focus on multidisciplinary education.

28. Gender Inclusion Fund for equitable education.

29. Special Education Zones (SEZs) for disadvantaged regions.

30. Balvatika: Pre-school education for children aged 3-6.

Higher Education

31. Multidisciplinary universities and colleges.

32. The Gross enrollment ratio (GER) in

higher education will reach 50% by 2035.

33. Four-year undergraduate programs with multiple exit options.

34. Academic Bank of Credits (ABC) for credit accumulation and transfer.

35. Multidisciplinary Education and Research Universities (MERUs).

36. National Research Foundation (NRF) to boost research.

37. Flexible curricula with creative subject combinations.

38. Integration of vocational education in higher education.

39. Internationalization of education: Foreign universities will set up campuses in India.

Teacher Education and Training

40. Online and distance learning to be expanded.

41. National Educational Technology Forum (NETF) for tech integration.

42. Single regulator: Higher Education Commission of India (HECI).

43. Phased out affiliation system for colleges.

44. Focus on adult education and lifelong learning.

45. Promotion of Indian languages in higher education.

46. Multiple entry and exit points in degree programs.

47. Integrated teacher education programs.

48. National Testing Agency (NTA) for standardized entrance exams.

49. Focus on employability and skill development.

50. Promotion of open and distance learning (ODL).

51. Minimum qualification for teachers: 4-year integrated B.Ed. by 2030.

52. National Professional Standards for Teachers (NPST).

53. Continuous Professional Development (CPD) for teachers.

54. Teacher vacancies are to be filled in a time-bound manner.

55. Promotion of local teachers in rural areas.

56. Use of technology in teacher training.

57. Mentorship programs for new teachers.

58. Focus on multidisciplinary teacher education.

59. Special training for teachers in foundational literacy and numeracy.

60. Teacher eligibility tests (TETs) to be strengthened.

Technology in Education

61. Digital infrastructure for all educational institutions.

62. Online learning platforms like SWAYAM and DIKSHA.

63. Virtual labs for science education.

64. AI-based learning tools for personalized education.

65. Coding and computational thinking from an early age.

66. Digital literacy for students and teachers.

67. E-content in regional languages.

68. Use of technology for assessments.

69. Promotion of open-source educational

tools.

70. Online degree programs for higher education.

Equity and Inclusion

71. Gender Inclusion Fund for equitable education.

72. Special Education Zones (SEZs) for disadvantaged groups.

73. Focus on education for girls and transgender students.

74. Scholarships for economically weaker sections.

75. Inclusive education for children with disabilities.

76. Promotion of Indian Sign Language (ISL).

77. Support for gifted and talented students.

78. Education for tribal and rural communities.

79. Focus on reducing dropout rates.

80. Equitable access to quality education for all.

Vocational Education

81. Vocational education from Grade 6 onwards.

82. Integration of vocational education with mainstream education.

83. Partnerships with industries for skill development.

84. Internships and apprenticeships for students.

85. Focus on employability and entrepreneurship.

86. National Skills Qualifications Framework (NSQF).

87. Vocational training for adults.

88. Promotion of local crafts and skills.

89. Recognition of prior learning (RPL).

90. Skill development centres in schools and colleges.

Assessment and Evaluation

91. Shift from rote learning to competency-based assessments.

92. Formative and summative assessments.

93. 360-degree holistic progress card.

94. Reduction in high-stakes board exams.

95. Focus on critical thinking and problem-solving.

96. Regular teacher training on assessment practices.

97. Use of technology for assessments.

98. Peer and self-assessment by students.

99. Continuous evaluation of student progress.

100. Focus on learning outcomes rather than marks.

NEP 2020 is a visionary roadmap for transforming India's education system. Teachers play a pivotal role in implementing these changes and shaping the future of education.

The National Education Policy (NEP) 2020 is a revolutionary plan to transform India's education system into one that is more open, comprehensive, and future-ready. It stresses "equal access to quality education" and encourages "critical thinking, creativity, and multidisciplinary learning" over "rote memorisation."

The 5+3+3+4 structure of the NEP 2020 curriculum emphasises basic literacy, vocational training, and flexible learning paths to ensure that students are well-prepared for the challenges of the 21st century.

Teachers play a crucial role in this change. They are not only teachers but also "facilitators of change. " It is their job to help students develop their skills, learn ideals, and create a love of learning that will last a lifetime.

According to NEP 2020, teachers must undergo continuous professional development

(CPD) to ensure they have access to up-to-date teaching methods, technology, and knowledge from various fields. Teachers can use student-centred approaches to create learning spaces that are enjoyable, welcoming, and engaging.

Teachers are also crucial for implementing the NEP's concepts of multilingualism, cultural integration, and vocational education, as well as closing gaps in quality and access, especially for the excluded. By following the guidelines of NEP 2020, teachers can equip their students with the tools they need to become critical thinkers, problem solvers, and responsible global citizens, which will ultimately contribute to India's better future.

II

Pictorial Representation on #NEP 2020

Interdisciplinary Learning in NEP 2020

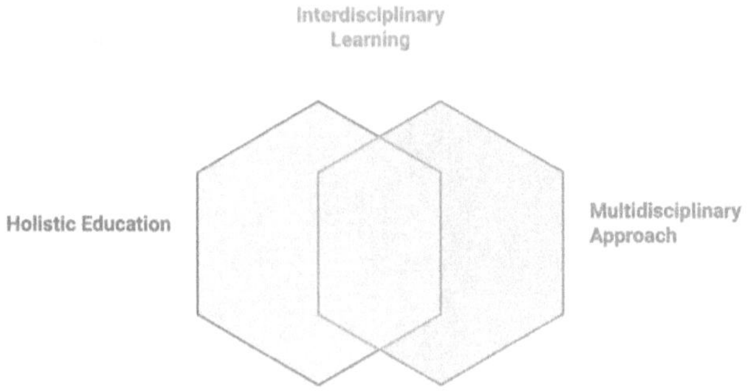

Integrating Technology in Education

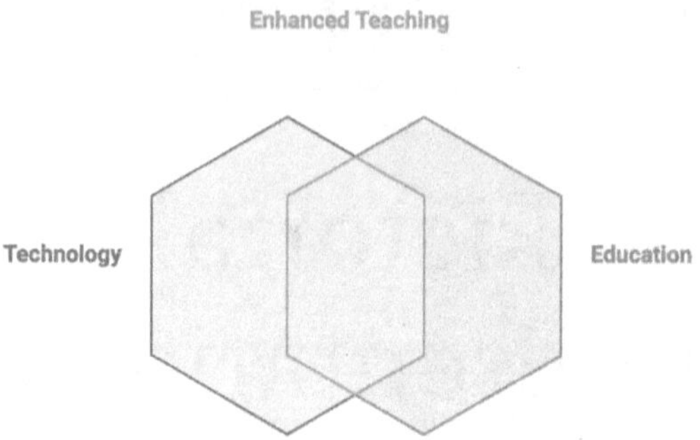

Pathways to Career Readiness

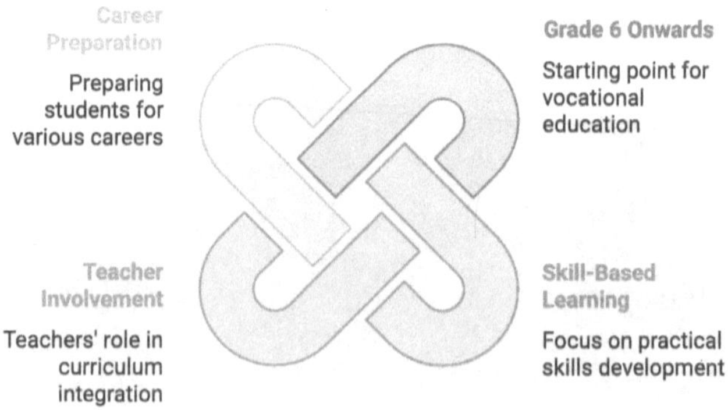

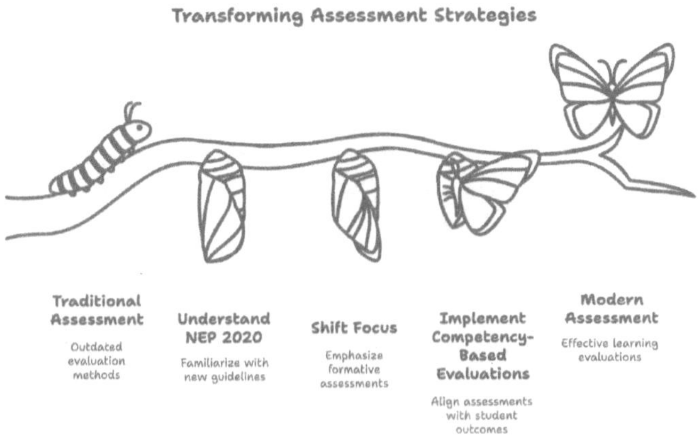
Transforming Assessment Strategies
Traditional Assessment
Outdated evaluation methods
Understand NEP 2020
Familiarize with new guidelines
Shift Focus
Emphasize formative assessments
Implement Competency-Based Evaluations
Align assessments with student outcomes
Modern Assessment
Effective learning evaluations

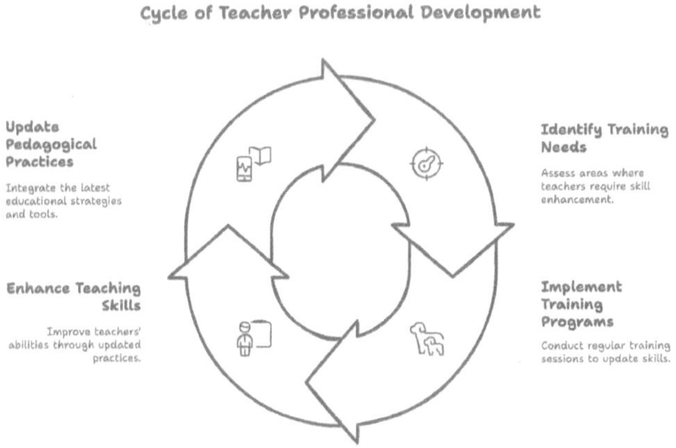
Cycle of Teacher Professional Development
Identify Training Needs
Assess areas where teachers require skill enhancement.
Implement Training Programs
Conduct regular training sessions to update skills.
Enhance Teaching Skills
Improve teachers' abilities through updated practices.
Update Pedagogical Practices
Integrate the latest educational strategies and tools.

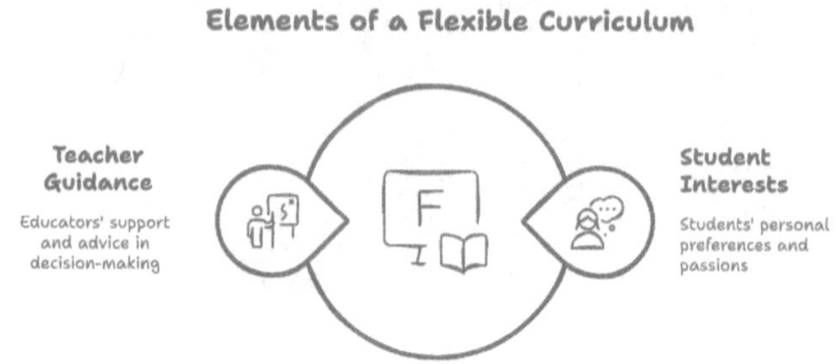
Elements of a Flexible Curriculum
Teacher Guidance
Educators' support and advice in decision-making
F
Student Interests
Students' personal preferences and passions

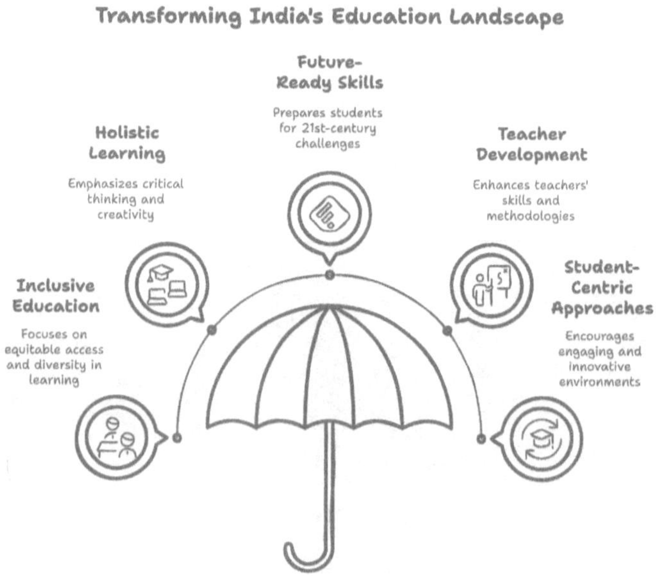
Transforming India's Education Landscape
Future-Ready Skills
Prepares students for 21st-century challenges
Holistic Learning
Emphasizes critical thinking and creativity
Teacher Development
Enhances teachers' skills and methodologies
Inclusive Education
Focuses on equitable access and diversity in learning
Student-Centric Approaches
Encourages engaging and innovative environments

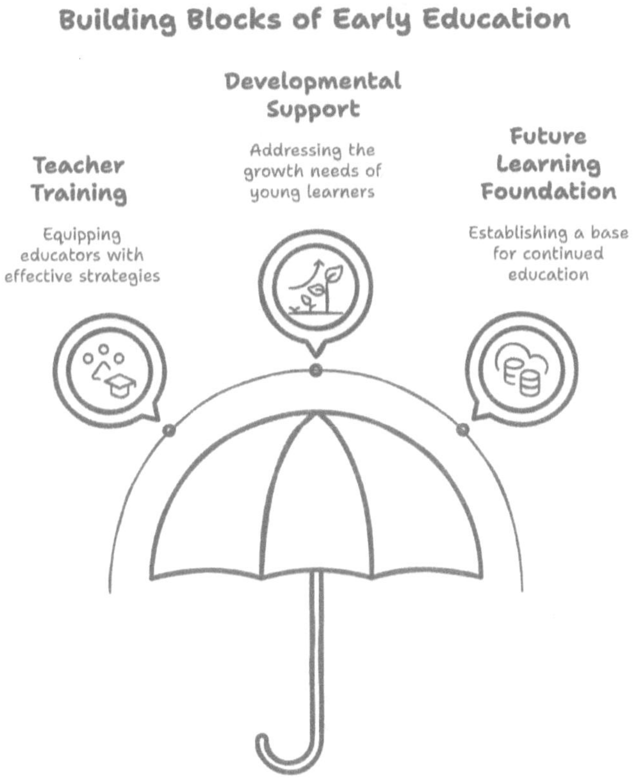
Building Blocks of Early Education
Developmental Support
Addressing the growth needs of young learners
Teacher Training
Equipping educators with effective strategies
Future Learning Foundation
Establishing a base for continued education

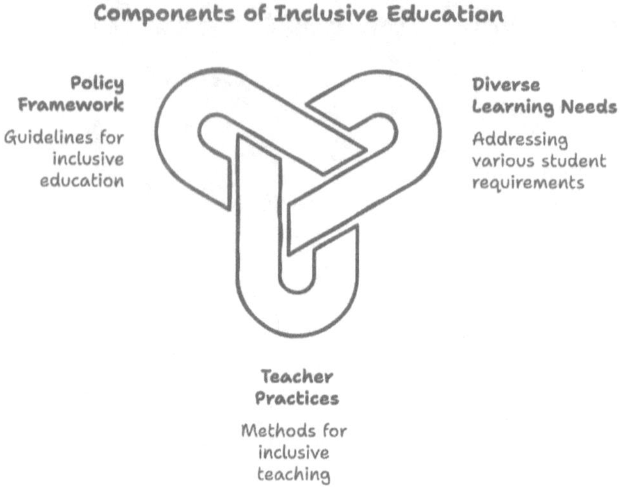
Components of Inclusive Education
Policy Framework
Guidelines for inclusive education
Diverse Learning Needs
Addressing various student requirements
Teacher Practices
Methods for inclusive teaching

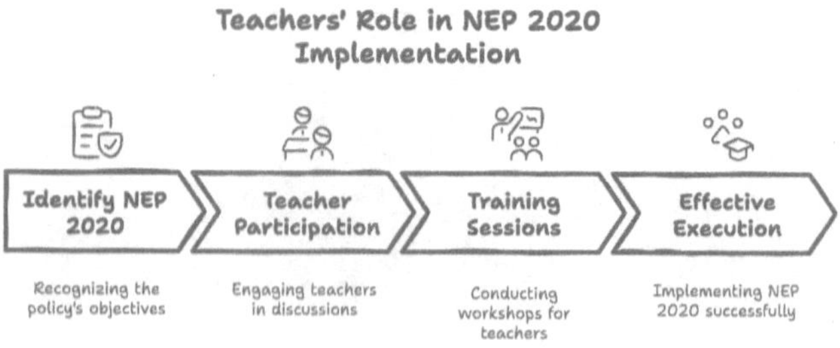
Teachers' Role in NEP 2020 Implementation
Identify NEP 2020
Recognizing the policy's objectives
Teacher Participation
Engaging teachers in discussions
Training Sessions
Conducting workshops for teachers
Effective Execution
Implementing NEP 2020 successfully

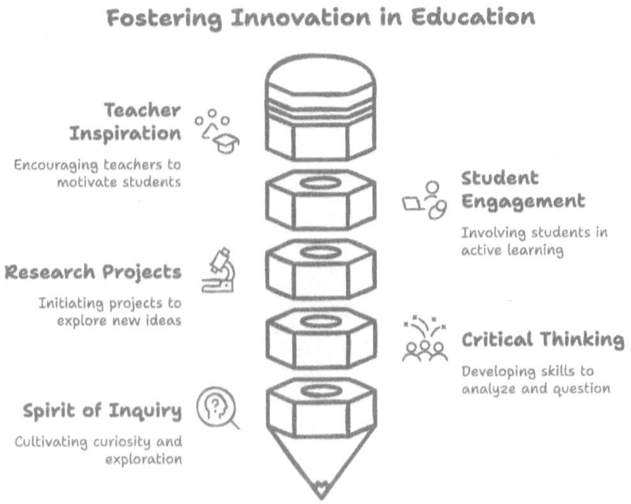
Fostering Innovation in Education
Teacher Inspiration
Encouraging teachers to motivate students
Student Engagement
Involving students in active learning
Research Projects
Initiating projects to explore new ideas
Critical Thinking
Developing skills to analyze and question
Spirit of Inquiry
Cultivating curiosity and exploration

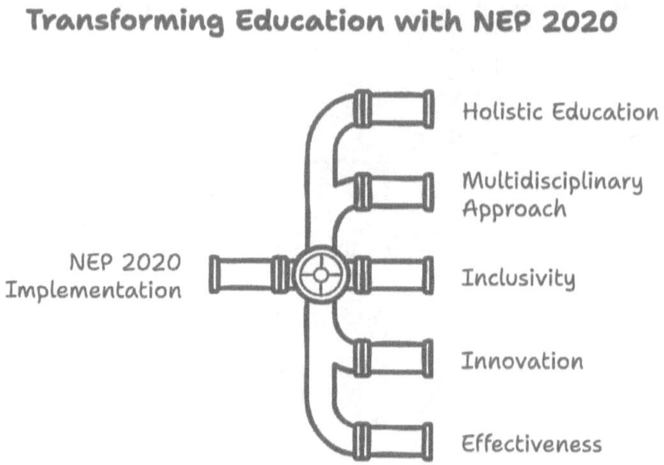
Transforming Education with NEP 2020
NEP 2020 Implementation
Holistic Education
Multidisciplinary Approach
Inclusivity
Innovation
Effectiveness

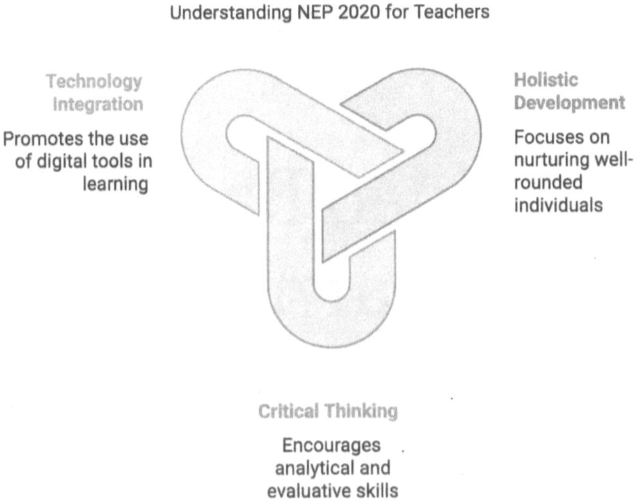
Understanding NEP 2020 for Teachers
Technology Integration
Promotes the use of digital tools in learning
Holistic Development
Focuses on nurturing well-rounded individuals
Critical Thinking
Encourages analytical and evaluative skills

III

Video Based Learning

Scan the following QR Code:

IV

Implementing NEP 2020

ONE: Start with awareness workshops.
Set up orientation workshops for all instructors and staff to ensure they fully comprehend NEP's philosophy, organisation, and significant changes, including the 5+3+3+4 system and holistic education.

TWO: Check Current Practices
Please review the current curriculum, assessments, teaching methods, and school culture to determine how they align with (or diverge from) NEP goals.

THREE: Make the Curriculum More Flexible
Add electives, modules that cross disciplines, and project-based courses so that students can pick subjects from other streams.

FOUR: Focus on Foundational Literacy and Numeracy

(FLN)
Reading, writing, and basic math should be the main things taught in the early grades. To make sure that all students meet FLN targets, use targeted interventions and ongoing benchmarking.

FIVE: Use active and experiential teaching methods.
Instead of teaching by rote, use inquiry-based learning, hands-on projects, field trips, and simulations to help students learn through hands-on experiences.

SIX: Start teaching in more than one language.
Use the child's home language for lessons in the early grades, at least until the fifth grade. After that, slowly include regional and other languages.

SEVEN: Combine Vocational Education Early
Start teaching skills and vocational modules in Grade 6, connecting real-world skills to schoolwork.

EIGHT: Align with the NSQF/Skill Frameworks.
Use the National Skills Qualifications Framework to map vocational and skills courses at the school level, ensuring they are recognised and standardised.

NINE: Continuous Professional Development (CPD) Set up frequent, ongoing cycles of teacher training (not just one-time workshops) to help instructors learn new ways to teach, assess, and use technology.

TEN: Encourage learning together and peer observation.
Encourage teachers to observe one another, plan classes collaboratively, and reflect on what they've learned

together. This promotes shared skills and new ideas.

Eleven: Use Technology and Mixed Learning
Use online resources, digital tools, adaptive learning platforms, and virtual laboratories to help with what you learn in class.

Twelve: Ongoing and Formative Evaluation
To keep track of how well students are performing, avoid giving them stiff annual tests. Instead, give them quizzes, portfolios, peer/self-evaluation, and other types of continual assessments.

Thirteen: Learning Paths and Timetables That Are Flexible
Create timetables that allow students to work on projects, complete internships, take remedial classes, or engage in extra work at their convenience.

Fourteen: Make groups or complexes of schools.
I'd like you to collaborate with schools in your area to share resources, best practices, and knowledge among teachers, as well as access to laboratories.

Fivteen: Getting parents and the community involved
Get parents, local businesses, and community members involved in the school's vision, vocational initiatives, and hands-on learning support.

Sixteen: Upgrade to better resources and infrastructure.
Please make sure that classrooms have the necessary physical and digital infrastructure, including libraries, maker spaces, labs, and internet access.

Seventeen: Bringing together local knowledge and culture
To make learning more relevant and meaningful, incorporate local arts, indigenous knowledge, environmental studies, and cultural history into the curriculum.

Eighteen: Helping and mentoring new teachers
Pair new teachers with experienced mentors who guide implementation of NEP-aligned practices.

Nineteen: Monitoring and feedback loops based on data
Monitor key metrics, including student learning, instructor adoption, and resource utilisation. Reflect on your actions and make adjustments as necessary.

Twenty: Support student voice and leadership
Let students help shape how learning occurs by providing feedback, suggesting projects, and participating in school governance.

Twenty One: Pilot Innovations Before Scaling
Test new pedagogical or assessment methods in a few classes, learn from the lessons, and then scale them across the school.

Twenty Two: Share success stories and celebrate small wins.
Recognise teachers who innovate, share case studies internally and externally to build momentum and belief.

Twenty-three: Promote Lifelong Learning / Adult Education
Utilise evening/weekend programs, or online modules, to upskill teachers, community members, or out-of-school

youth.

Twenty Four: Link with Industry / Vocational Partners
Forge partnerships with local industries for internships, guest lectures, real-world projects, and vocational exposure.

Twenty Five: Champions & Change Agents
Identify enthusiastic teachers/leaders as NEP champions who lead by example, influence peers, and drive change in their teams.

A Note To Educators

A Plan for Schools to Follow NEP 2020

Schools need to start with training for all teachers and staff to make sure everyone understands the National Education Policy (NEP) 2020's concept, framework (5+3+3+4), and focus on holistic development. The next stage is to examine our current practices—curriculum, teaching methods, and assessments—and ensure they align with the goals of the NEP. Schools should make their curricula more flexible by adding electives, interdisciplinary modules, and project-based learning opportunities. At the same time, they should focus on Foundational Literacy and Numeracy (FLN) in the early grades through targeted interventions and regular benchmarking.

Learning should change from rote memorisation to active, hands-on, and multilingual methods. This will encourage inquiry-based learning, vocational integration starting in Grade 6, and alignment with the National Skills

Qualifications Framework (NSQF). Teachers need to continue learning and collaborating with their peers, and technology-enabled blended learning and formative evaluations can support this process.

Flexible schedules and learning paths can include projects, internships, and extra help with learning. School complexes also promote the sharing of resources and best practices among schools. Involvement from the community, including parents, local craftspeople, and businesses, can enhance vocational exposure and regional relevance. Schools also need to invest in improved infrastructure, digital tools, and content that aligns with their cultural context.

A culture of continuous improvement is fostered by providing guidance and mentorship to new instructors, utilising data-driven monitoring, and celebrating success stories. To maintain momentum, schools should encourage student voice, test new ideas before rolling them out to all students, and support staff members who serve as NEP champions.

Ultimately, making the school responsible for lifelong learning and adult education, while collaborating with businesses to provide real-world learning experiences, would render NEP 2020 a dynamic framework for change. These phases work together to create schools that are ready for the future, inclusive of everyone, and filled with new ideas. They are what the NEP is all about.

Scan the following QR Code to watch the video on

Implementing NEP in schools.

The roadmap I've included outlines the necessary steps for schools to successfully implement the National Education Policy (NEP) 2020. Implementation begins with awareness workshops for staff to ensure a thorough understanding of the new 5+3+3+4 structure and its associated philosophy, followed by a review of existing curriculum and assessment practices. Key pedagogical shifts involve moving learning from rote memorisation to experiential, multilingual, and inquiry-based approaches, alongside the crucial prioritisation of Foundational Literacy and Numeracy (FLN). The roadmap also stresses the importance of continuous professional development

(CPD) for teachers, incorporating technology and data-driven monitoring, and integrating vocational education with community and industry partnerships. Ultimately, these actions aim to foster inclusive, innovative, and future-ready schools by ensuring alignment with the spirit of the NEP.

BOOKS BY THE SAME AUTHOR

www.ingramcontent.com/pod-product-compliance
Lightning Source LLC
Chambersburg PA
CBHW020513160726
47991CB00007B/2928
9798897440450